With Sincere yoos

Frank A. Driskill

595

Davy Crockett

The

Untold

Story

Frank A. Driskill

EAKIN PRESS ★ BURNET, TEXAS

FIRST EDITION

Copyright 1981
By Frank A. Driskill

Published in the United States of America
By Eakin Publications, P.O. Drawer AG, Burnet, Texas
78611

ISBN 0-89015-298-5

ii

DEDICATION

To my granddaughter
Stephanie Driskill

ACKNOWLEDGMENTS

An attempt to evaluate Texas history is not complete without an understanding of the role Tennessee played in the birth and the development of the Republic for which David Crockett, her native son, gave his life.

Had there not been a Tennessee then, there might not be a Texas now. We salute the Volunteer State and send our sincere appreciation.

Further recognition belongs to those who have helped make this new account of Crockett's life in Texas possible. Encouragement has come from many directions but only a few can be recognized.

Adelia Neu has done an outstanding job editing the material. She helped put the dialogue in the language of the times to give the story a more realistic flavor.

Stephanie Driskill, my granddaughter, read the manuscript to evaluate its appeal to young readers.

Billy Joe Thomas supplied material about the Crockett family in Granbury. He also furnished the picture of the burial site of Elizabeth Crockett and two of her children (Acton State Park).

Noel Grisham has offered continued encouragement by stressing the need in the public schools for new material on David Crockett and his life in Texas.

The people in Crockett, where I grew up have given freely of the information there along with their encouragement.

TABLE OF CONTENTS

INTRODUCTION

The part of the Davy Crockett story that covers his life in Tennessee follows the record as closely as possible. The dialogue, on the other hand, is fictional.

The Texas story, as it is presented here for the first time, has been handed down by members of the Gossett family.

Crockett's experiences in Texas, as told by A.W. (Andy) Gossett and members of his family, differ from other published accounts of the same period. They, in turn, differ from each other. The only possible source that can be considered accurate is an alleged diary that may have been found among Davy's belongings by a Mexican officer after the fall of the Alamo. The finding of a diary may, or may not, have been true.

Accounts of Crockett's activities in his so-called autobiography frequently differ from other published records. He may have taken certain liberties to create a greater interest. Davy Crockett was an expert storyteller.

There is reason to believe the Gossett story. Mrs. Betty Gossett, a third generation member of the family, had letters that indicated Crockett had spent the time in East Texas at the places named in this story and during the time he is given credit for.

Andy Gossett, a professional surveyor and former neighbor of Davy Crockett in Tennessee, is the focal point of this presentation. Many of the land patents in Nacogdoches and Houston counties, as recorded in the General Land Office in Austin, show they were surveyed by A.W. Gossett.

Mrs. Betty Gossett passed the Davy Crockett story along to this author many years ago and showed the letters that seemed to indicate its accuracy. She was seventy-five years old at the time.

The story is recorded here for those who may enjoy Crockett lore from a new approach.

Frank A. Driskill

THE ALAMO...where Davy lost his life.

EARLY TENNESSEE CABIN.

I

A Young Boy Grows Up

"I didn't shoot that big gobbler," Davy Crockett told Rebecca Shaw. "I got us a fat hen."

He had slipped out of the cabin before daylight and quietly made his way to the brush pile on the hill. From there he could watch the turkeys roost on the creek and would be ready to shoot when the wild birds flew down to feed.

"Soon as I eat, I'll dress 'er out."

"That old gobbler'd been too tough. He's been chasin' them hens too long," she answered with a smile. "Rather have a hen any day." Then she continued, "Sam promised to try to get back by Thanksgiving and that's tomorrow. Shore hope he makes it. I got punkin pies baked last week. The sweet taters and apples are cookin' now and with turkey and dressin' we'll have right good eatin.' That's a lot to be thankful for."

Rebecca Shaw watched Davy as he hurried through his breakfast. She hadn't forgotten the tall, skinny boy who had knocked on the door over a year ago. It had been near freezing that night and a slow drizzle was falling. It was a night not fit for anyone to be traveling.

She remembered digging through a box and

finding some clothes her married sons had outgrown.

"Use that corner room and get into these dry clothes," she had told him. "Bring me the wet ones and I'll dry 'em out. While you're changin I'll get you some food."

She began filling a plate with squirrel stew from the stove and added some corn pone. "Here, eat this, son. You'll feel better when you get your belly full."

Sam Shaw, Rebecca's husband, had been lounging in a homemade rocker by the fire. He was about half asleep and spoke for the first time.

"It's too cold out fer you to be movin' around. The boys' room is empty and you're welcome to stay a spell."

The smile on Davy's face, between bites of stew, gave them the answer.

Sam Shaw continued, "What's yore name, son, and where you from?"

Davy stopped eating long enough to answer. "My name's Davy. Davy Crockett. I've come from over Tennessee way. My papa runs an inn and tavern out of Nashville a few miles."

"You've come a long ways from home, son."

"I reckon so," Davy answered quickly, "but mama and papa had nine of us kids and feedin' us ain't easy. I thought I'd like to get away a spell and have a look around."

Rebecca Shaw had watched Davy's face as he talked. "You're shore you just didn't run off?" she asked him.

He hung his head before he answered. "I reckon I did jest that, ma'am." Then he added as he looked up and smiled, "Guess I'll be goin' back 'fore long 'cause my folks will be a needin' me."

There was a softness in Sam Shaw's voice as he spoke. "Want to tell us about it, son?"

Davy seemed pleased to talk to the kind people. "Well, I'm fourteen and I ain't had much schoolin'. Until last year there weren't no school to go to so I could learn my letters. When we moved and papa took over the inn, he sent us younger kids to a school nearby. He and mama was dead set on us kids learnin' to read and write.

"I wuz doin' good—real good until I whupped a bully in a fight. He had been jumpin' on little kids so I whupped him good. The schoolmaster had a rule that to stay in school after a fight you had to take a thrashin'. Papa said I had to stay in school, so I jest run off. Come to Virginny with a wagon train what had stopped at the tavern. The wagon-master tried to work me without payin' me so I run off from him. That wuz about three days ago and I've been in the woods huntin' a place to go."

Sam Shaw was satisfied. "Winter'll be here 'fore long, son, and I kin use some help here on the farm. You need to settle in 'till warm weather, so how about us makin' a trade? You'll get yore keep fer helpin' me and I'll throw in a rifle to boot. Won't be long 'till you'll be needin' yore own shootin' iron."

Davy's face lighted up at the mention of a rifle. "You got yoreself a trade," he said, shaking hands with the older man.

Davy Crockett liked the Shaws immediately. Mrs. Shaw reminded him a bit of his own mother, who also was named Rebecca. She treated him like he was one of her own sons.

She made clothes for him, replacing the ones he continued to outgrow. "You're growin' like a weed and bustin' out at the seams," she told him one day.

At night after the chores were done, they all would sit in front of the fire and she would teach Davy how to form his letters on the big slate her two boys had used.

"You're a smart boy, Davy," Rebecca Shaw frequently told him. "You'll be somethin' one of these days when you get yore schoolin'."

Sam Shaw treated Davy like a man. They hunted together and it wasn't long until Davy learned how to set trap lines for small animals. Before long he could handle a rifle and shoot as well as Sam could.

"One of these days you'll be knowed all over fer the way you handle a rifle," Sam complimented him.

Davy smiled. "I aim to try. A man about lives by his rifle in these parts."

The older man continued his advice. "You need to be careful. A rifle ain't no plaything. Remember, when you're fightin' Injuns, don't shoot 'till you see the whites of their eyes."

A frown came over Davy's face. "Papa's folks wuz killed by Injuns. I reckon I ain't got much use fer them varmints."

Sam answered quickly, "There's a lot of good Injuns. A mightly lot of 'em. You'll learn that as you go 'long. But while you're movin' around learnin', be shore you find out which ones ain't."

Almost two years passed before Davy made the move to go home. It wasn't until a wagonmaster he'd known came by the Shaw farm that he finally decided to make the journey back to see his folks.

Telling the Shaws he was leaving wasn't easy. There was a lump in his throat and tears in his eyes when he bade his friends "good-bye."

"I'll get my schoolin'," he promised them. "When I do, I'll send along a letter. 'Fore then I'll send word down the trail ever chance I get."

Davy reached the inn on August 17, his sixteenth birthday. When he walked into the lobby carrying his rifle, no one recognized him at first. He had changed so much and his younger brothers were more interested in the rifle than who he was.

"Davy—Davy," his mother exclaimed as she came out of the kitchen and saw him. "You've come home—You've come home." She hugged him and then backed away to take another look. "You're a man now. I done lost me another boy, but we're shore glad you're home."

John Crockett, Davy's father, tried to hide his joy at seeing his son, but he couldn't. As he hugged him with one arm, he said, "You've growed as tall as I am. Livin' in the woods has done you good."

Davy had been uncomfortable not knowing how his family would react to his returning home. It relieved him when he realized they were proud to have him back.

"How things been goin', papa?" Davy asked.

"Tolerable. Jest tolerable. Yore two brothers what married has left me short-handed and I done run up a debt I ain't paid 'cause I ain't had the money."

It didn't take Davy long to get back to the chores and his schooling. The new schoolmaster was the son of an old Quaker who owned a store nearby. Davy worked around the school to pay for his lessons and helped out at the store to pay his father's debt.

With the debt paid after a year, Davy stopped working at the store and spent his free time in the woods. Rebecca Crockett had two milk cows, some chickens, and a garden, so with the game Davy brought in, she was able to serve heartier meals to the hungry travelers.

Besides hunting, Davy set trap lines for mink and fox. He caught many animals and soon traded the skins for a larger rifle.

"I need me a rifle so's I can kill me a bear," he told his father one day. "I had some bear meat in Virginny and you jest can't beat it. Mama will really be packin' folks in when I start bringin' in 'em bears."

He was eighteen when he traded the skins for a new rifle. This was the same year he started calling on Polly Finley, whom he had met in school. A year later, after working hard for his father and supplying wild game for his mother to serve, Davy asked Polly Finley to marry him.

II

Davy Crockett Starts His Family

On August 14, 1806, three days before Davy
Crockett's nineteenth birthday, he married Mary
Finley at her parents' home. Davy and Mary set out
the next day, with the rest of the wedding party,
which included two of his brothers and a sister, for
the Crockett inn to visit the rest of his family and
friends who had been waiting to welcome the newly-
married couple.

Until her marriage, few people knew Mary
Finley's Christian name. She had been called Polly
all of her life and it didn't take long for her new
friends to pick it up again.

Davy rented a cabin and a small farm from the
Quaker store owner. The old man liked hard working people and Davy had pleased him while he was
paying off John Crockett's debt.

Polly Crockett received two cows with calves
from her parents, which helped the young settlers.
After Davy finished the chores on the farm, he did
extra work for the Quaker to earn enough to buy a
plow horse. Later he traded the skins from the
animals he trapped for two young colts.

The friendly Quaker allowed the young couple
to purchase supplies at the store until harvest time.
They worked hard on the farm for several years and

CONGRESSMAN DAVID CROCKETT

their first two children, John and William, were born there.

The Quaker store owner was largely responsible for the first move the Crocketts made. One day he remarked: "Thee'll never be a farmer, I fear, but perhaps thee'll become the greatest hunter in the West."

Davy was quick to accept the thought. "I want my boys to grow up in a new country," he told the Quaker, "and to learn to hunt. It's huntin' I want to do myself, so it's best we be gone."

The language of the woods was something Davy Crockett understood. He liked people and liked to go to parties, to dance, and to tell stories, but the area was getting too crowded for his comfort.

Polly was as adventurous as Davy, so the daring couple decided to move to some undeveloped land over the Cumberland Mountains in southern Tennessee. Part of their trip deeper into the state was made by boat on the Holston River and on into the swifter waters of the Tennessee, covering many winding miles that cut through mountain spurs until they reached the Elk River country. From there they went overland to where they wanted to settle.

Arriving in time for the planting season, Davy bought some cleared land at the head of the Mulberry Fork that was a branch of the Elk River. The other settlers, scattered over a wide area, helped them build their cabin.

Davy found the new land to be fertile and with plenty of game. It wasn't long until he was recognized as the best bear hunter in the area. He continued to bring in the big animals and was the envy of his neighbors who seldom had the luck to shoot at a bear. The big bearskins were used as rugs to cover the dirt floors of the cabin. Davy was proud and enjoyed showing other settlers his accomplishments.

Polly made clothes for Davy and the boys from the deerskins he brought in, as well as the moccasins they wore. She made coonskin caps, which soon became one of Davy's trademarks. There was little reason for Polly to get involved in spinning and weaving, but her Irish pride caused her to weave some cloth to make the cabin more livable and attractive.

Deer and turkey were plentiful, as well as smaller animals. Davy was able to trade some of the skins and wild meat for supplies needed by his family. The old Quaker had been right. Davy Crockett wasn't much good at farming, but he was gaining the title as the best hunter in Tennessee.

Their third child, a daughter, was born in the Elk River country. She was named Margaret after Davy's sister, but it wasn't long until she was called "Little Polly." After her mother's death, she became known as Polly.

It wasn't long until Davy was restless again. Game was becoming increasingly scarce and more settlers were coming into the territory. The idea of moving had been on his mind for some time, but he needed something to give him an extra push. This push came in the form of a hurricane which took the roof off the cabin and twisted the rafters that had been holding it.

"I don't believe we will stay here any longer," he told Polly. "There's gettin' to be too much of a hotchpatch of people about. I crave to go where there is wilder land and more game. Over south near the mountains there's good soil in the thick of huntin' country. I think I'll like it over there, I'll go build us a cabin. Then I'll come back to get you and the children and we'll take our plunder and be on our way. We've been here over two years now and that's long enough."

Polly and the children were ready to go. Davy

sold his land for fifty dollars and bought a small tract near a deep stream further south and deeper into the forest. Before winter set in, he had the cabin built and his family moved. The new location was near the boundary of the Mississippi Territory.

The Indians in northern Alabama and southern Tennessee were becoming restless. Five tribes—the Creeks, the Cherokees, the Chickasaws, the Choctaws, and the Seminoles were beginning to feel the pressure of the white man as the frontier moved westward.

The Creek Nation was the first to move against the settlers and Andrew Jackson was sent with a detachment of soldiers to put down the uprising. Davy Crockett volunteered, but from the beginning he was at odds with the general over the Indian question. During the conflict, Davy met Sam Houston, another patriot who would also figure in the future history of the then little known country called Texas.

Polly didn't want Davy to join the Jackson troop, but again her Irish pride served her well. As she brushed back the tears she told him, "You do what you feel in your heart is right. The children and I will make out 'til you get back."

After the Creek War, the Crocketts enjoyed a brief period of happiness. Hunting was good and Davy collected a large supply of fine furs. Meat was plentiful and again he used it in exchange for gunpowder, lead, and other supplies they needed. Things were better than they had ever been until Polly suddenly became sick and died.

Davy never recovered from her loss. After placing the limestone slabs over her grave in the forest, he was ready to move on. He moved, with his children, deeper into the wild country, settling on land near another large creek that was eighty miles further west.

Polly's death came in the summer of 1815 and after the move, Davy asked a younger brother and his wife to come live with him to help with the children and the chores. It didn't take long, however, to realize the new arrangement would not work. It was then that Davy decided he needed to marry a second time.

III

A Second Marriage and a New Career

Davy soon met Elizabeth Patton, a large and attractive woman whose physical capacity to work was greater than that of most women. Being the young widow of James Patton, who had lost his life in the Creek War, she was living on the attractive little farm she and her deceased husband had acquired. She was from a prominent family in North Carolina, also named Patton, but there was only a remote possiblity that the two families were related.

Elizabeth became Mrs. David Crockett in the summer of 1816. The area where she and Davy were living at the time was later to become Franklin County, Tennessee. They adjusted well to each other, making this a good marriage. Reports indicate that she had several hundred dollars in reserve, which served as an asset as the couple continued to move further west.

Civilization began to push Davy Crockett again. He set out on exploring expeditions in Alabama and further west into Tennessee. In the fall of 1816 a committee headed by Andrew Jackson negotiated a treaty with the Chickasaw Indians for territory in the southern part of the state, east of the runoff from the Tennessee River. For this reason, Davy, after exploring in several directions, brought his family to an area that was supplied by water from what was known as Shoal Creek, later to be a part of Lawrence County.

The Crocketts lived well for two or three years without any law except that the settlers set up for themselves. At one of the meetings Davy was appointed a magistrate and later was named a court referee.

Davy Crockett became known for his fairness and his objectivity. His popularity made the people more than willing to entrust the court cases to him.

In talking about it later, he explained, "My judgments were never appealed; but if they had been, they'd have stuck like wax. I gave my decisions on the principles of common justice and honesty between man and man. I relied on natural born sense, not on law, for I had never read a page in a law book in my life."

David Crockett's popularity was revealed when he was elected a colonel in the local militia regiment. He defeated a captain of the unit that served the area where he and Elizabeth had been living for only a short time.

The next step for the "Canebreak Philosopher," which he was later to be called, was in 1820 when he was elected to a seat in the Tennessee legislature. This was an early indication of the strength of a rural democracy that was to elevate Andrew Jackson to the office of president of the United States.

In the summer of 1825 Davy Crockett ran for and was defeated for a seat in the United States Congress by the incumbent, Colonel Adam Alexander, a man of considerable means and a friend of Andrew Jackson. The colonel agreed with the future president that "high tariff" was the answer to an economic security for the young nation. The price of cotton was high at the time and Colonel Alexander, in his campaign speeches, projected the reason as being the tariff protection it was receiving.

Later when the bottom dropped out of the cotton market and prices reached eleven cents a pound, Davy decided to try again. In the second race, he competed against Colonel Alexander and also General William Arnold, who had somehow managed to become the only major general in the Tennessee militia. The prospects for a victory for Davy didn't look promising until fate took a hand.

On speaking tours all three candidates were on the platform at the same time, but Colonel Alexander and General Arnold tried to ignore Davy Crockett when possible. At one meeting, General Arnold answered all of Colonel Alexander's charges, but did not address a single remark to Crockett.

While the general was speaking, a flock of guineas came to the edge of the clearing, making so much noise that he had to stop until the fowls were driven away. When the speech finally ended, Davy arose quickly and loudly addressed the general.

"The general is the first man I have ever known, other than myself, who understands the language of the fowls."

When asked what he meant, Davy continued: "Since the general has not had the politeness to mention me in his speech, my little friends, the guineas, have come up and started to cry, 'Crockett, Crock-ett, Crock-ett.' The general has been ungenerous enough to have them driven away."

The crowd took up the chant, "Crock-ett, Crockett, Crock-ett" and the word spread up and down the backwoods trails. In August, the polls showed a clear victory for David Crockett.

The accounts of David Crockett's three terms in Congress are filled with question marks and contradictions. Even Davy, himself, in his

15

autobiography, made statements that do not always agree with the congressional records.

It is clear, however, that Davy (he was called Davy by his colleagues although officially his name was recorded as David) was at odds most of the time with his old commander, Andrew Jackson. Their basic differences were land policies and the handling of Indian treaties that were continually being broken by the United States government.

Davy had fought the Red Men on more than one occasion, but many Indians had fought on the side of the white man against other Indians. Davy had lots of friends in all of the civilized tribes and it rubbed a raw spot on his mind to see them taken advantage of.

Davy Crockett was a popular member of Congress. His story-telling ability and sense of humor made him the center of attraction when members got together. And on more than one occasion, he managed to turn antagonism into surrender by resorting to some of his homespun expressions.

A congressman from New York was opposing the land bill Davy had introduced, but was being kept off balance in his arguments by a series of questions by Crockett. Finally, the New Yorker lost control of his temper.

"The congressman from the canebreaks seems to know little about his own bill," he said, "or he wouldn't ask so many questions."

Davy received recognition from the Speaker and smiled as he spoke: "My colleague from New York what has about done run off all the Injuns, should know a body needs to ask questions now and then. He shore ought to know it ain't safe to buy a pig in a poke unless you kin at least see a curly tail."

A low rumble of subdued laughter had to be brought under control by the Speaker's gavel. The tension was broken and the congressman from New York sat down.

Although Crockett felt a deep sense of loyalty to the people he represented, life in Washington was not to his liking. He spent as much time as he could with Elizabeth and the children in the Tennessee woods. A trip into some of the little known areas in search of bear would break the tension and he would feel normal again.

Things reached a turning point in the summer of 1835. The power of Andrew Jackson was brought into play and Crockett was defeated in his bid for reelection. It was their continuing differences over land law that finally brought a showdown. It is ironic, however, that John Wesley Crockett, Davy's oldest son, later became a member of Congress, and in 1841 was successful in passing the law that had caused his father's defeat.

Just how Davy Crockett accepted defeat is not clear, but his immediate reaction is a matter of record.

"I'm seceding from the Union," he told Elizabeth when he returned home and greeted her. "I'm gonna look for new land and a new home for us. Sam Houston wants me to join him in Texas. There's free land to be had down there and Sam needs me to help him out. I'll get us a place and come back fer you and the children. Woman of mine, I'm goin' to Texas."

GENERAL SAM HOUSTON
...Davy missed his appointment with this friend.

IV

Davy Crockett Leaves For Texas

"Betsy" was Davy Crockett's pet name for his wife. He had given it to her when they first met. His friends in the congressional district gave him a beautiful new rifle in appreciation for his work and he also named it "Betsy."

"This ain't no jumped up affair, this here trip to Texas," Davy told his wife as he set about to get his gear together. "Sam is pushin' me to join him—you know, Sam Houston. We wuz in the Creek War together."

Betsy Crockett knew her husband. She knew he was a determined man who would do what he thought was best. "When you say 'Be sure you are right and then go ahead,' you mean it, don't you Davy? I had as soon have you in Texas as in Washington. That's 'cause I'd rather live in Texas when you get settled and come back for me and the kids."

"I'll be back. You know I'm comin' back. Sam writes that Texas is great country. He's met a man from Louisiana by the name of Jim Bowie, who's married to a Spanish señorita from San Antonio. In Sam's letter he told me, 'Jim Bowie does a lot of things different from me but he knows the truth about Texas and he ain't afraid.' I figger if Sam

19

knows folks like Jim Bowie it might be a right good place to go."

Elizabeth Crockett was patient. "I take it Sam Houston don't like Washington any better than you do.

"Maybe not as good. Didn't stay but one term. Then he took off and run for governor of Tennessee. Got elected—remember? Then the woman he married messed him up and he pulled out and left for Texas. Set up a law office in a place called Nacogdoches, or some such name. I ain't jest sure what it is since I ain't never heard it pronounced."

To get a final reaction, Elizabeth asked, "Will you miss anything about Washington?"

He thought a minute. "Some. Maybe more'n I think right now but I can't figger whut it'll be. I shore can tell you whut I won't miss."

His wife waited without saying anything and he continued: "I don't like the way them folks dish out the truth in little packages," he said. "Some of them folks—up in high places too—wouldn't recognize the truth if they met it head-on in the middle of a narrow road. And some of those city folks would climb a tree to tell a lie when they could stand flat on the ground and tell the truth."

"Just city folks?" Elizabeth Crockett was more relaxed than she had been when they had first started talking.

"Yea, city folks. Us people from out in the woods may not know as much, but we don't have to lie about it." Then he grinned. "Maybe that's the reason we don't lie. We ain't so learned we have to lie. I hate liars, Betsy, you know that."

Davy's wife was overly concerned about her husband going alone into an unknown territory, but she did not want him to know it. One day she casually asked, "You tried to get anyone to go with you?"

20

"Yep, I shore have. I asked four or five and could of had all the company I want if I'd jest wait 'till harvest's in. We ain't got no harvest to speak of and you and the kids can handle whut there is. I'd like to have company, but I ain't in no mood to wait.

"You know any folks in Texas 'ceptin' Sam Houston?" Betsy asked, thinking of Davy being in a land of strangers.

"Andy—Andy Gossett is there, accordin' to Sam's letter. Him and his family. You don't know Andy, but he lived over by papa's inn when I first started out. Later we wuz together durin' the Creek uprisin'.

"Sam says Andy and his folks has been livin' in Texas a couple of years now. He's a surveyor fer the government and has been layin' down a bunch of new lines around there. Sam says I may want to settle near where Andy is. It's still in Nacogdoches County, a place called Caney Creek."

August 17 was always an important date in Davy Crockett's life, his birthday. Things seemed to happen to him on this date. August 17, 1835, dawned bright and clear and Davy was ready to pull out for Texas.

The saddle bags on his big black gelding were loaded with gunpowder and sheets of lead. He had a supply of rifle balls, but he carried a bullet mold and extra lead, for use later.

In a big bedroll tied to the back of his saddle, he had three pairs of moccasins, two buckskin suits, and an extra coonskin cap. A pot for boiling coffee, two tin cups, and a skillet were in a bucksin bag tied to his saddle horn. The coffee and other supplies were in another bag on the other side. A bearskin coat, tied over his bedroll, completed his gear.

"I jest might run into some unfriendly Injuns," he told Betsy, after he decided not to take a pack horse. "Big Bill don't need to be slowed down none

21

and he kin outrun any of 'em Injun ponies if I give him his head. I don't need nothin' I ain't got on my saddle noway."

He mounted and looked back toward the house. "Havin' my scalp hangin' from a totem pole wouldn't exactly happy me up," he said, as he turned in the saddle. Then he waved to his wife and children. "I'll be back 'fore you know it," he called out as he rode away.

Davy got an early start so he could cover familiar territory early in the day. Entering new territory would slow him down as he needed to feel his way beyond the familiar hunting area. He also knew it would be necessary to watch for Indian signs.

Moving along in the woods was easy for Davy and Big Bill. Staying off the beaten trails would be safer, he knew, and it wouldn't slow them down enough to notice.

As he rode along in the woods, Davy felt a presence of another person before he actually read the signs which told him he was right. He knew the other rider was not an Indian because the horse had been shod. The tracks were deep, indicating it was a big horse or with a heavy load.

A short distance away, Davy spotted the horse's head. The rider was waiting behind a clump of trees near a creek bank.

As Davy moved forward, the rider came into the open area. Davy stayed astride Big Bill, holding his rifle across his saddle in case he needed to use it.

"Howdy, stranger. My name's Jed—Jed Roberts. I rode in from down on the Alabama line.

"My name is Davy Crockett."

The stranger's face brightened. "I've heard of you. You're knowed about as a great bear hunter. Where you headin'?"

"Texas. You ever heard of a territory called Texas?"

"Yep, I shore have. It's down below the Arkansas line. That's where I'm goin', back down in the Arkansas country. Been there twice already."

Davy relaxed as he answered, "I'd heard that's where it is. I'm aimin' to join Sam Houston down there."

Jed Roberts got down off his horse. Wanta eat? I got some beef jerky," he said. "We might set a spell and brew up some coffee."

Davy hesitated. "What about Injuns? Any Injuns around to smell the smoke?"

"Not likely. As I said, I've come this way before. Injuns don't move this high up, fer as I ken tell."

"I'm ready fer coffee," Davy told him.

"Me too. Didn't fix none earlier. Didn't want to take the time. We'll rest a spell and then take turns watchin' each other's back as we go down the trail."

Davy Crockett smiled. "Sounds like you know what we got to do to get to Arkansas territory. I'm right proud to have you to ride with."

Davy's Trip To Texas

V

Texas At Last

Jed Roberts was a good man in the woods. He had more education than most and could read signs as well as any Indian. Davy Crockett felt confident with Jed since he had been down the Arkansas trail before. They made a good traveling team, having developed a deep respect for each other.

Some days they covered long distances, scarcely stopping except to water and rest their horses, or for a bit of food. Other days they traveled short distances as they stopped to fish or hunt for some fresh meat to eat.

"I'd like a young squirrel cooked over a hot fire," Jed told Davy, "but my rifle is too big fer killin' squirrels. I'd rip 'em to pieces."

"A good squirrel would be mighty fittin'," Davy replied. "I'll see about barkin' us some. Shore lots of 'em around."

"Bark us some?" There was a puzzled look on Jed's face.

Davy's eyes danced as he said, "Yea—somethin' I learnt. You don't need no small gun and you don't need to mark 'em up neither. I knock the bark right off the limb what's under 'em. Down they fall right out of the tree and I grab 'em as quick as they hit the ground. Then I knock the heads agin my rifle stock."

One day Davy brought in four squirrels and Jed grinned. "Not a mark on 'em," he said. "Now I done learnt me somethin' new."

They made camp early that day and talked while the squirrels were cooking. "You ever heard of a feller by the name of Austin?" Jed asked. "Steve Austin, he's called."

"Sam mentioned him in a letter I got. Down in Texas now. Wuz head of things in Texas fer a time until he got throwed into prison in Mexico."

"I knowed him in the Arkansas Territory," Jed said. "Wuz a territory judge out of Washington."

Davy reached over his shoulder for his deerskin pouch and took out a well-worn piece of paper.

"Sam sent me a map," he told Jed. "I didn't figger on runnin' into you else I'd have used it 'fore now."

He spread the map on the ground where the bright light of the fire would enable them to see the lines. "Where you think we've got to?" Davy asked.

Jed looked at the map a minute before he answered. "Here's the Mississippi River. I figger we'll be there in a couple of days. I remember this spot 'cause I camped here before."

He ran his finger along the line on the map that was the Mississippi River. "I been meanin' to talk to you about yore trip when we hit the river. Me, now I take a boat downstream a ways and you oughta go on even further. We'll need to use the river all we kin. Shore will save time and rest the horses too."

Davy kept looking at the map. "It figgers. Sam said that. I jest been wonderin' where you're leavin' me. Shore hate to see it come about, myself."

There was a strong feeling in the look Jed gave Davy. "Me, too, I hate it bad. Maybe I'll be down Texas way and look you up after you bring yore family and get settled. Since I don't have no family, I'm liable to be anywhere."

Jed looked at the map again. "Right here is where the Arkansas River runs into the Mississippi. I'll leave you there and ride across to a little settlement where I got some friends. You'll need to stay with the boat another day 'till you hit a little place on the Mississippi side called Vicksburg. You kin get a barge across to Louisiana Territory and ride to a Injun town called Natchitoches. It's sittin' on the Red River clean across the state, but you ain't fer from Texas then.

The trip to Vicksburg was a new experience for Davy, but he missed Jed Roberts more than he cared to admit. Usually he was self sufficient and content within himself when he was in the woods, but Jed had penetrated his cover and reached down deep inside of him. He would always think of Jed as a lasting friend.

There was a trading post across the river from Vicksburg and Davy stopped there to get supplies. Later he had to walk back several miles to get a bottle of horse liniment. Big Bill had stepped into a gopher hole and sprained his right front foot. It was a bad sprain and would take time to mend. Davy decided to make camp on a little stream and start caring for the horse he loved.

"I ain't goin' a step without you," Davy said aloud, as if the animal could understand. The low neighing sound from Big Bill seemed to indicate that he did. "We done come along too fer together to split up now. Sam and them folks kin wait 'till yore foot is well."

Davy camped on the bank of the little stream for two weeks. He rubbed the liniment on the sprained foot several times a day. Then when the swelling seemed slow in going down, he dug red clay from the side of the hill and mixed it with boiled water and liniment. He smeared the thick paste as a poultice around the injured foot and wrapped it with a piece of buckskin. As the mixture cooled, it drew the swelling out.

"Shore wuz a good thing we could get this liniment," Davy said, again speaking to Big Bill. "I'd shore had a lot of walkin' to do if we hadn't been close."

Big Bill was like a part of the family and family was important to Davy. He had written Elizabeth from Vicksburg, telling her about his trail friend, Jed Roberts, and of his travel plans on toward Texas. Included in his letter were personal messages to each of the children as Davy felt this was a way to keep close relationship with them while he was away. The ones born after his second marriage were too young to fully understand, but they were included anyway.

When they broke camp, Big Bill could put his weight on the injured foot, but it was still too tender to carry a rider. Davy replaced the bridle with a rope halter he always carried. Their early progress was slow, but as they moved along, the ankle got stronger and the pace was increased.

It took fifteen days to reach Natchitoches which was roughly 125 miles, as the crow flies. Then Davy Crockett was able to relax again. Big Bill's foot was good as new. Davy was anxious to move on because he knew it wouldn't be long until he would be in Texas with his old friend, Sam Houston. He stayed overnight camped on the Red River, got fresh supplies, and left early in the morning.

Since Big Bill's accident, Davy hadn't stopped long enough to hunt or fish. He had several chances to kill a deer, but he passed them up because he couldn't keep the meat.

"Don't ever kill nothin' you can't eat nor give

away," he remembered telling his sons. "Leavin' meat to spoil is a sin."

Big Bill seemed to sense that Texas was near. He became impatient and Davy had to hold him back. When they reached the Sabine River, the boundary between Louisiana and Texas, it was just before sundown. Davy made camp and caught a mess of fish for supper. In his early years he hadn't fished much, but while he and Jed were on the trail together he acquired some of the patience required and he began to like it. He had come to like fish fried in corn meal and as he told Jed, before they parted, "Fishin' shore saves powder and lead."

The next morning Davy broke camp before daylight. "We need to get on across," he said out loud. "Looks like we gonna have to swim the river, boy, but that ain't no problem. When we do we'll be in Texas."

VI

Davy Crockett Finds The Gossetts

Some of Davy Crockett's anxiety was lost when he reached Nacogdoches six weeks after he had left home. He learned that Sam Houston had left for the little South Texas village of Goliad where the Texas forces had captured a Mexican supply depot the week before. Davy met a man, Adolph Sterne, who seemed to be in charge of the stone fort there. It was Sterne who told him about Sam Houston.

"Sam's been lookin' fer you fer a month," Sterne told him. "A messenger wuz through here some time back and told you were headin' down this way. Sam couldn't wait no longer so he took off fer a meetin' that likely will end up with our folks declaring independence from Mexico. Things been headin' that way fer a spell now and Sam's liable to end up runnin' things since Steve Austin's gone east to try to get money to buy supplies."

Davy seemed deep in thought. "You figger we'll end up in a war with Mexico?"

"Shore looks that way. Them Meskins ain't gonna give up easy. They've seed this comin' and already pulled in their horns. They called our Mexican commander here at the fort, Colonel Piedras, back to San Antonio. He is one good Meskin and I hated to see him go. If this thing gets heated up and

ADOLPH STERNE AND
his home in Nacogdoches.
Davy Crockett visited with
this early day Texan before
leaving for the Battle of the
Alamo.

spreads I shore hope I don't have to look at him over my rifle sights."

"Whut chances we got?" Davy asked. "Ain't they got a mighty lot of men?"

Adolph Sterne smiled. "They'll outnumber us about five to one but I'm figgerin' that's about even."

A tall, gaunt red-faced man with big ears and a long nose had been listening to the conversation and turned to Davy Crockett. "Shore they got us outnumbered, colonel, but we kin whup them Meskins with cornstalks."

Davy Crockett grinned. "Maybe we kin, my friend, but do you reckon we can talk them Meskins into fightin' with cornstalks?"

After signing the oath of allegiance to Texas at the stone fort, Davy Crockett visited around for a few days. There was a lot of activity at the outpost and excitement ran high concerning the upcoming break with Mexico. Nacogdoches was at the crossroads and people moving in all directions brought news to the fort.

It didn't take Davy long to get restless again although Sam Houston had left word for him to wait until he returned.

"Anybody know Andy Gossett?" Davy asked at the fort.

"Shore thing," a man answered. "I run into him further over in the county a while back, layin' down some survey lines. Lives over on Caney Creek," he told me. "Here I'll draw you a map what'll get you there."

A few days after Davy arrived in Nacogdoches he wrote his wife again.

"The country here is a land what gets a hold on you" he wrote, "and won't let go. It's a lot like Tennessee in some ways but it's got more timber and pine trees what are taller and straighter. They grow

31

so thick you don't hardly see no daylight when you're in the woods. I ain't tried it yet but I don't hardly think I could shoot through the woods without hittin' a tree."

"Sam ain't here. He'll be back 'fore long and left word fer me to wait. While I'm waiting' I'm goin' out a ways and find Andy Gossett. Folks here know him and say he don't live more'n three days away.

"This is fine country and I like it. Plan to look around when I find Andy. We jest might settle right close to him so we kin visit. I hear tell a lot of folks from Tennessee is comin' in."

"Soon as things get straightened out and settle down I'll get Andy to help me and I'll file on what land we'll be allowed. Then I'll come fer you and the children. You can bet the Crockett name is gónna be a good one in Texas."

Davy ended the letter with some personal remarks and gave it to Adolph Sterne to put on the stage.

The next morning before the first light, Davy Crockett saddled Big Bill and rode out to find the Gossetts. When he located them at the end of the third day, Andy Gossett greeted him warmly. "Heard you wuz comin'. Sam Houston sent word a ways back. Thought maybe you'd bring some men with you, though."

"Would have," Davy replied, "if harvest had been over. Don't know whut Sam thought 'cause I didn't say nothin' about no extra men. Some of 'em should be comin' 'fore long and I'll meet 'em at the fort."

Davy stayed with Andy and his family until after Thanksgiving to help with the harvest and bring in fresh meat. He then became restless again and left for Nacogdoches even though a riding preacher had reported that Houston had assembled

OLD STONE FORT in Nacogdoches.

a small army and was at Goliad.

Word then reached Davy in Nacogdoches that Houston would not be back soon because with the way things were moving, it was time to strike in force if Texas was to be free.

Already there had been skirmishes near San Antonio at a little outpost called Gonzales and then at Goliad where Sam Houston had gone. The patriots turned back Mexican soldiers who had tried to take the one cannon they possessed. At Goliad the Texas forces overran the Mexican supply depot and captured a quantity of rifles and supplies.

The Mexican General Santa Anna was moving northward to join his advanced forces with the intention of smashing the Texas resistance before it could be consolidated into a real force.

When news of the South Texas activity reached Nacogdoches, Davy Crockett could hardly contain himself. "Where's Sam," he almost shouted. "Sam ain't jest sittin' around and I shore need to be with him. If I knowed where to find him, I'd take off."

Sam Houston was moving around trying to raise an army and secure supplies. He hoped to cut Santa Anna off before he could overrun San Antonio. A patriot whose name was Ben Milam had come up from Mexico to help the Texas cause. He had originally helped Mexico gain her independence from Spain, but didn't like the way the settlers in Texas were being treated. He was ready to lead Texas forces outside the settlement against the advance guard of Santa Anna's forces who were in control of the Alamo, an old Spanish mission in the heart of town. Milam was killed during the siege, but the Mexicans in the Alamo ran up the white flag of surrender.

This battle action took place on December 4, 1835, and gave Sam Houston more time to organize and reinforce his troops. His headquarters were at

San Felipe, the capitol of Austin's colony, and from there he dispatched a letter to Davy Crockett in Nacogdoches.

San Felipe-Texas Territory
December 8, 1835

Dear Friend Crockett:

You no doubt feel hard toward me because of my slow reponse to your arrival in Texas, especially since you came at my constant urging.

My slowness in acting has been based on events over which I have had no control. At this time I see our future with a little more accuracy. You definitely will be a valued part of my plans now that I may be able to give you some guidance in joining me.

Our initial stand will be in San Antonio where a band of Texans captured a mission there called the Alamo. This happened only a few days ago and I shall dispatch garrison troops to occupy the mission as soon as possible.

My apologies to you for my neglect. Had anyone told me Davy Crockett would be in Texas this long without a visit from me I would have put him down as a liar. Not so, my friend. The Mexican mind functions in strange ways and the proud and arrogant Santa Anna cannot believe we will be a threat to his powerful forces. He expects to tramp us into the ground with no quarter given.

Santa Anna will not win. His arrogance and greed will be his undoing. Besides, right and justice are on our side. We will not meet him on the field of battle until we select a spot that is advantageous to us.

Our course of action may call for hit and run tactics and even retreat before we establish a position we feel is favorable. Let me assure you I have no hesitancy in retreating if it is to our advantage, but I will never surrender. Death is far more desirable and with much more honor.

Friend Crockett, I ask of you to dispatch with haste word to our friends in Tennessee. Encourage those who are in sympathy with our cause and willing to fight for it, to join you in Nacogdoches. Your responsibility is to bring these men to the Alamo. This will be our first line of defense, and hopefully, all we will need.

Your devoted friend,
Sam Houston, General
The Army of Texas

Houston's letter reached Nacogdoches on December 15, 1835. It was as if an anvil had been lifted from his shoulders after Davy read it. Quickly he got a letter off to Elizabeth to contact the men he had talked to about joining him in Texas. "Tell Bob Campbell I'm countin' on him," he wrote her. "They need to leave as soon as possible and come to the stone fort here. I'll either be at the fort or waitin' at Andy's."

Adolph and Eva Sterne tried to talk Davy into spending Christmas with then, but he declined.

"Andy Gossett's expectin' me over there," he told them. "I promised him afore I left. Andy is busy with his farmin' and his surveyin' and he don't have time to hunt. I need to help him get some meat for Christmas."

"I'll be back," Davy told his friends at the fort. "As soon as we get things settled down country, I'm comin' back and file on some land. Shore hope it ain't long either. I ain't never heard of this place Sam calls the Alamo, but it'll do as good as the next place fer whut we got to do."

Davy Crockett left the stone fort in Nacogdoches on December 16, 1835. It took him two days to cross the Angelina and Neches rivers and cover the wooded land that extended to Caney Creek. Big Bill was rested and he moved as fast as Davy would let him go.

VII

A Last Visit With The Gossetts

"I wuz hopin' you'd make it back fer Christmas," Andy Gossett told Davy when he rode in from Nacogdoches. "The kids been askin' if you wuz comin'. They want to hear more of your yarns."

Davy laughed. "I got plenty of 'em, it looks like. Ain't run out yet."

As Davy got off Big Bill he handed Andy a big sack. "On the way over here I run into a man whut robs bee trees and done a little tradin' with him. Wild honey will go mighty good fer Christmas."

"Shore will, Davy. Maud and the kids will be mighty pleased. Me too."

Davy Crockett showed his friend the letter from Sam Houston. "What's back of all this, Andy? Why can't folks get along with one or another, as big as this country is?"

The surveyor thought a minute. "Maybe several things. Religion, fer one. Maybe not the big thing but it shore has helped."

Davy looked puzzled. "Religion?"

"Yea, they got a law down here what says you can't practice anything but the Roman Catholic belief to own land in Texas. Course that's all the Meskins practice anyway. The law wuz made when this country belonged to Spain and it ain't been changed."

"Now you take Sam—Sam Houston. When he got here he had himself baptized a Catholic so he wouldn't run into no problems. He jest figgered it would be simpler to join up. Likely he'll do somethin' else when we get free."

"What about this feller, Steve Austin, who seems to have been runnin' things? Does he go along with such a law?"

"He don't like it but he's had to try to enforce it to get along with them Mexico City folks. He even went down there to try to get a few things cleared up and Santa Anna had him throwed in a dungeon. He stayed fer over two years and nearly died. That shore didn't help none up here."

Andy Gossett was a surveyor in Tennessee and the Mexican commander in Nacogdoches appointed him to serve in East Texas Territory. He traveled a lot and was able to keep up with what was going on all over the state.

The Gossett home was the crossroads for travelers. A stagecoach line ran about 18 miles south and travelers came through on their way to catch the stage. Most of them had a message for Andy. Frequently it was a message to pass on to someone else but "The Overground," as it was called, worked well—at times better than a letter.

Andy continued to talk to Davy about the problems the white settlers were facing. "You got to remember one thing," he told him. "It ain't the Meskin people livin' in the territory what's causin' the trouble. They are fine folks and want to be free from Mexico as bad as we do. We wouldn't have no trouble if it wuz jest them."

"I noticed a few Meskins around Nacogdoches," Davy replied. "Talked to a couple of 'em. They seemed real sociable."

"They are. These are the ones what stayed around when the garrison officers wuz pulled out. They mix well and like our way of doin' things," Andy continued.

"What about further down the country?" Davy wanted to know. "How they feel 'round San Antonio?"

"The same way. It's that way all the way to the border. There's lots of Meskins what wuz born in Texas. They are as proud of their heritage as we Anglos are. Maybe more so 'cause they see whut goes on in Mexico and they know it ain't good."

"If a fight starts up, whut will these folks do?" Davy kept pressing the issue.

"Some of 'em will try to stay out of it, fer one reason or another, but a lot of 'em will join up with us. There's done been some leaders what's come over to our side. I keep hearin' about a man named Zavala. He wuz involved in the fight agin' Spain and later turned up as one of the governors of Mexico. He didn't like whut was happenin' up here so he shucked it all and become a colonist hisself."

"I heard about him at the fort. His name come up the other day. Another man too, a feller named Seguin. Seems like he's got pretty high up on the pole."

Andy Gossett smiled, "Yep, they is both good hosses. This Seguin feller has put together a whole outfit of native Meskins to fight fer Texas. I hear he aims to join up with Sam Houston to fight Santa Anna."

"You read Sam's letter. They'll stop Santa Anna but I shore would like to get him in my sights. I'm hankerin' to get on down there." From Davy's tone it was evident he felt he knew the outcome.

Andy changed the subject. "Maud's about got

the vittles ready so we better go wash up. We kin talk later."

The four Gossett children were fighting to sit next to "Mr. Crockett" so Davy settled it by letting them draw straws.

"You kin take turns after this," he told them.

The meal was nearly over before Andy spoke. "Maybe we need to go into the woods fer game, Davy?" he said. "The smokehouse ain't got much left in it and with Christmas comin'—well, we jest need to do some huntin'."

His wife, Maud, spoke up: "Truth is, Andy's been waitin' fer you to come showin' up. He figgers we'll have a lot more to eat if you are doin' the shootin'."

Davy Crockett laughed. "Me and Andy belong together. He can do the farmin' and I can do the huntin'. Right now hits the huntin' what needs to be done."

"Bring us some turkey feathers," the children called out all at once. "We want to play Injun."

Maud Gossett was more practical. "I need to make a new feather duster. The one I got is worn down to the stumps."

The men hunted for two days and came back with both horses loaded. "We hit a lick," Andy told Maud as they walked up to the kitchen door.

There were plenty of turkey feathers for a new duster and the children to play Indian. When the meat was dressed, which included a wild hog they had come across by accident, the smokehouse was full and overflowing.

"It won't stay that way long," Andy said. "We'll share with our neighbors; and the way folks stop by here, it'll mostly be gone by spring."

Late the next evening a rider pulled up at the gate and called out. Andy went to the door. "Set down, stranger," he replied, "and come put the feed bag on with us."

The man was a Methodist riding preacher by the name of William Stevenson. "I'm out of Arkansas Territory. Been down here preachin' on the sligh—in folks' homes. Been doin' right good, too. The Mexican officials who are natives don't care, and them out of Mexico are too far away and too busy.

"Seems that way," Andy replied. "Fore he left, Colonel Piedras let some folks hold a camp meetin' right out in the flat open."

"I know, I know," Reverend Stevenson replied. "We'll get the religious question worked out 'fore long. A body ought to be able to worship the way he wants to and we'll keep pushin' that way."

Christmas was only three days away and Andy tried to get the minister to stay, but he refused. "I'll make it home by Christmas Day," he told him.

Davy enjoyed the Gossett children on Christmas, but he missed his own. He especially missed Elizabeth.

"If Betsy and the kids could of been here it would be a lot better," he told Andy. "By next year maybe we'll all be together again. Right now, though, we best think about the liberty of Texas."

VIII

For The Liberty of Texas

After the skirmishes at Gonzales and Goliad, the situation began shaping up for Sam Houston. He could see the necessity of a declaration of independence from Mexico and a final showdown on the field of battle to guarantee it. Houston devoted the months of November and December of 1835 in an attempt to set in motion the forces necessary to meet the challenges that lay ahead.

Even after Ben Milam and his forces had driven the Mexican troops out of the Alamo, San Antonio remained in a state of unrest. The native Mexicans, loyal to the Texas cause for freedom, knew it would be only a matter of time until Santa Anna would move his headquarters from Laredo and personally lead the drive to avenge earlier defeats his troops had suffered.

Sam Houston had originally planned to meet the Mexican army on the plains below San Antonio, but the possibility of a flanking operation by a surperior enemy force caused him to change his plans. He also realized the Texas forces were so scattered that it would be impossible to pull them together as a unit on such short notice. A second plan, which called for a delaying action until he could maneuver the enemy into a more desirable battle sight, was his next choice.

New people supporting the Texas cause continued to surface. One was William B. Travis, an attorney from South Carolina, who had come into the territory to practice law. He had already seen action against the Mexicans at Anahuac, located at the mouth of the Trinity River above Galveston; and had helped to organize a small army that had driven the enemy from Texas soil.

It wasn't long, however, until the Mexicans were back around San Antonio in increasing numbers. The little towns in the area were soon overrun and it became evident that more action was needed to protect the settlers. It was fitting, then, that Travis, with the flame for freedom in his blood, was sent to join Jim Bowie at the Alamo.

Sam Houston's letter to Davy Crockett to meet him in San Antonio had been in good faith, but his plans had to be changed. Neither he nor Colonel Fannin, who had 500 troops at Goliad, were able to reach the Alamo since Mexican lines surrounded the city. Travis and his small garrison at the Alamo were left in a dangerous position.

Travis dispatched Juan Seguin and Antonio Arocha to see if help could be found. Because of their knowledge of the language and the customs of the enemy, the colonel felt they could slip through the Mexican lines if anyone could. Their efforts to get help failed and only a few individuals answered the call. The only other reenforcements to get through were Davy Crockett and the men from Tennessee.

Sam Houston, in the meantime, had left his little army at a safe encampment and journeyed to Washington-on-the-Brazos. Here he signed the Declaration of Indpendence from Mexico on March 2, 1836, his forty-third birthday. With all hope of joining Travis at the Alamo gone, Houston returned to his army to map the strategy that would enable him to meet Santa Anna on favorable terms.

Bob Campbell and eleven volunteers from Tennessee rode into Andy Gossett's yard on January 20, 1836. Davy Crockett was there and greeted his friends. They stayed that night to rest their horses and replenish their supplies.

With Davy Crockett leading them toward San Antonio, he called for a rest about twenty miles from the Gossett farm. "The horses need more rest," he said, "before we settle down to hard ridin'. It shore wuz too much too expect Maud Gossett to cook fer this crew and she'd done it if we'd stayed. I jest thought we'd come out a ways and make camp on our own."

They camped under a large oak tree on the side of a hill. Nearby was a spring of clear water that boiled out from underneath a rock ledge and ran down a slight incline into a creek below.

"This shore is a pretty spot," Bob Campbell remarked. "I'll bet the sound of that water'll make us sleep good."

"You don't need nothin' to make you sleep, Bob," Davy told him. "It shore is pretty, though. Maybe when we come back this way I'll file on this land so I'll have that spring. Likely I ought to put up a sign now sayin' I camped here."

Crockett and the twelve Tennessee volunteers slipped through the Mexican lines and entered the Alamo on February 11, 1836. Bob Campbell had been unable to attract more men since most of them had families and they did not feel the heat from the fires for freedom that burned as far away as Texas. The arrival of Crockett and the Tennessee patriots brought the total force at the Alamo to 181 men with a few women and children.

Davy Crockett asked for Sam Houston when he

arrived and was surprised he wasn't there.

"He'll be here," Crockett told his men. "Sam wrote me to meet him here and Sam's a man of his word."

Colonel Travis, who had been listening to the conversation, was not so sure. He understood the problem facing Houston and had about given up on additional troops.

The situation at the Alamo went from bad to worse. Finally on February 24, 1836, Travis issued an appeal that would eventually be heard around the world. He concluded his strongly worded statement by saying:

If this call is neglected, I am determined to sustain myself as long as possible and die like a soldier who never forgets what is due to his own honor and that of his country.

William B. Travis, Colonel
Commander of the Alamo

The challenge went unanswered and help did not come.

It was March 6, 1836. A sentinel stood on the wall of the Alamo, peered into the darkness, and called another sentinel. "Go get Travis," he said.

Before the sentinel could move, a bugle sounded beyond the ramparts to the south. This was answered by another bugle to the west. A shot rang out from across the open field and two more shots answered.

The twelfth day of siege was soon to dawn and the forces under Travis had taken one onslaught after another. Each time the charge came they were able to drive the enemy back with heavy losses.

Once again the defenders of the Alamo, wiping sleep from their eyes as they poured out into the

DAVY USED ol' Betsy as a club...

darkness, swarmed like a nest of hornets as they answered a call never to be forgotten. Like hornets they stung as they turned back charge after charge from Mexican forces urged on by Santa Anna. He had mounted the blood red flag of *no quarter* and carried it himself.

The outcome became clear. As each wave of dead fell closer to the walls, those still living climbed high over the bodies of their comrades to mount the crumbling walls of the Alamo that had been torn by cannon fire.

Soon it was over. The last to go was Davy Crockett. He had no powder left and used Betsy as a club. He stood there, one arm useless. He had a deep gash in his cheek where he had been cut by a saber. At his feet were the bodies of many Mexicans who had falled in an attempt to reach him in hand-to-hand combat. His Bowie knife, a gift from Jim Bowie, had served him well.

The dawn had broken through with a gray beginning and the day seemed to get darker as the tragic end became a reality. The Alamo had fallen and Santa Anna, true to his word, put the garrison to the sword.

On March 27, three weeks after the fall of the Alamo, another tragic event made Sam Houston more determined than ever to bring Santa Anna to his knees. News reached him on Palm Sunday that Lieutenant Padilla of Santa Anna's army had captured a detachment of Texans at Goliad under the command of Colonel Fannin and had them executed. They were first taken outside of the little village and required to dig trenches.

"You will help with the slaughtering of some beeves," the soldiers were told. When the ditches were finished, they were all shot in the back and dumped into the holes, on top of each other. The incident is frequently recorded as "The Slaughtering of The Beeves."

Liberty for Texas came forty-five days after the fall of the Alamo. A little known place called San Jacinto on Buffalo Bayou was selected by Sam Houston to meet the superior Mexican forces.

Before he fought the final battle of the Texas Revolution, Sam Houston called his men together. "Men," he said. "If there are any here who shrink from the issue they need not cross the bayou. Some must perish, but it is for a glorious cause. Remember the Alamo! Remember Goliad! Victory or death! There will be no defeat. Victory is as certain as God reigns. Trust in the God of the just, fear not."

With 783 men, Houston faced his greatest challenge. He sent his trusted scout, Deaf Smith, to cut Vince's bridge across Buffalo Bayou so there could be no retreat. When Deaf Smith returned waving his ax and shouting "Vince's bridge is down," Sam Houston ordered the charge.

It was one of the shortest battles in history, lasting only twenty minutes. Santa Anna had fourteen hundred men but they were taken by surprise just as they were about to begin their siesta hour. In the confusion and flight, Santa Anna disappeared, but was soon captured wearing the uniform of a private soldier. One of his own men recognized him and gave him away with a salute.

From a pallet under a large oak tree, Sam Houston, who was confined there because of a wound, dictated the terms of the surrender, which included independence for Texas. The only thing that may have dimmed his enthusiasm was that his friend, Davy Crockett, was not with him to share the glory. Fate had dictated glory for Davy Crockett in another direction.

SAN FRANCISCO de los Tejas in Davy Crockett National Forest.

The hand fate had dealt Davy Crockett was not one he would have chosen. He had come to Texas at the urging of Sam Houston, but the two friends were not to meet.

Davy Crockett had set out to find new land and a home for his family, but this never came about. Instead of fighting beside his friend when it became evident fighting would be necessary, Crockett gave his life in a location he knew little about, and under circumstances he would have not chosen.

Even in death Davy Crockett was equal to the challenge. He was able to meet head on the fate that had been dealt him and with the other defenders of the Alamo, had given his friend, Sam Houston, the extra time he needed to write the final chapter in a proud history that few people, other than Texans, really understand.

EPILOGUE

After the fall of the Alamo, Davy Crockett received added attention in East Texas. Texas became a republic when the Declaration of Independence was signed at San Jacinto in 1836.

The next year, a new county was chartered from part of the Nacogdoches area and named for the hero of San Jacinto, Sam Houston. On December 29, 1837, a charter was issued for a county seat and named Crockett. It is located where Davy Crockett and his men camped on the way to the Alamo. The big oak tree where they camped is gone, but the spring still flows and a marker tells the story. Crockett is the fifth oldest town in the state.

To the east of Crockett is the 160,000-acre Davy Crockett National Forest. Within its boundaries is a replica of an old Spanish mission, San Francisco de los Tejas, built in 1690 as the first effort in the area by the Spanish to educate the Tejas Indians. Second only to Ysleta in age, the old mission is on the famous El Camino Real—"The Old San Antonio Road." This is the route Davy Crockett and his men used when they made the trip to San Antonio.

Ten years after the charter for Crockett was issued, Texas had joined the Union, and Elizabeth Crockett, with her younger children, came to the state. They settled in Hood County, which had as its county seat the historic and picturesque little town of Granbury. The record is not clear whether or not Elizabeth Crockett visited the town named for her husband, but she went to Hood County because her veteran's land grant was there.

Texas is the only state in the Union to be admitted by treaty. Statehood was granted in 1845 through a resolution by Congressman Milton Brown of Tennessee. Under the treaty, Texas was allowed to keep her public lands, but she was responsible for her public debt, which had reached in excess of ten million dollars.

With little cash and no credit, it became necessary for the Texas legislature to issue land certificates to be used as money. Over 37 million acres of public land were conveyed by special Headright Certificates to the survivors or the heirs of those who had fought in the Texas Revolution. It was one of these 320-acre grants that brought Elizabeth Crockett to Texas.

She died in 1860 and was buried in the Acton Cemetery, six miles east of Granbury. Later, two of her children were buried there.

The smallest state park in the country was created within the Acton Cemetery because of Elizabeth Crockett's death. To legally spend public money for a grave marker, it was necessary to make her burial site public property. In 1911 an act of the legislature called for the erection of a twenty-five feet statue of a woman looking out in the distance. The little park is twenty feet long and twelve feet wide. The official records in Austin list it as .006 of an acre.

The two families involved, the Crocketts and the Pattons, established roots in Hood County and descendants still live there, even though some have spread over the state. Ashley Crockett, a grandson of Davy Crockett, was a community leader and newspaper publisher in Granbury for many years. He sold his last newspaper in the mid-1930's, but remained in Granbury until his death in June of 1953. His daughter, and Davy Crockett's great-granddaughter, Mrs. Gladys Hendricks, still lives there.

STATUE IN Texas' smallest state park commemorates wife of Davy Crockett.

GRAVE MARKER for Elizabeth (Betsy) Crockett, wife of Davy Crockett, located in Acton Cemetery near Granbury.

BIBLIOGRAPHY

1. *The Life of Davy Crockett, An Autobiography;* Grossett & Dunlap, 1902, New York
2. *Davy Crockett, The Bravest of Them All who Died in the Alamo* by V.F. Taylor; Naylor & Company, San Antonio.
3. *Ten Tall Texans,* by Dan Kubiak; Naylor & Company, San Antonio.
4. *Davy Crockett,* by Constance Rowrke; Hartcourt, Brace & Company, New York.
5. *Davy Crockett, The Man and The Legend,* by John Shackford Pemberton Press; 1968, Austin.
6. *Davy Crockett's Own Story,* written by himself; Citadel Press; New York.
7. *The Texas Almanac,* 1980.
8. *Encyclopedia Britannica.*
9. *Told orally by Mrs. Betty Gossett.*
10. *Added material by Mrs. Gossett's daughter, Mrs. Harry Trube, Sr.*

INDEX

A

55